Mirage

A comedy

David Foxton

Samuel French — London
www.samuelfrench-london.co.uk

FOR AMATEUR PRODUCTION ENQUIRIES

UNITED KINGDOM AND WORLD
EXCLUDING NORTH AMERICA
plays@samuelfrench.co.uk
020 7255 4302/01

Each title is subject to availability from Samuel French,
depending upon country of performance.

CHARACTERS

Mr Desmond Borage
Mrs Pamela Borage (née Anstruther), his wife
Butters, a butler
Mr Gerald Fairfax
Mrs Evadne Fairfax, his wife
Mr Dinsdale Morton

The action of the play takes place in the living-room of Gerald and Evadne's country house

Time — late 1920s

AUTHOR'S NOTE

The play is a comedy of manners. It owes something to P.G. Wodehouse with a possible touch of Noël Coward. It is farcical but not a farce. It needs control and style; its pace should be precise, languid, measured and rarely hurried.

MIRAGE

*A country house somewhere in the English countryside. The
late 1920s*

*At the rear, french windows lead on to the garden. There are also
exits* L *and* R. *There is a chaise longue* C *and a chair* DR. *Drinks
including gin, tonic and whisky, and glasses are on a side table.
There is an occasional table on which a radio plays music of the
period*

*Pamela lounges on the chaise longue, almost reading a magazine.
She might toy with a cigarette in a holder. She looks at her watch
occasionally and off stage as though she expects someone to
arrive. Desmond, Pamela's husband, paces across the stage
awkwardly. His pacing sometimes coincides with the tempo of the
music. Something would seem to be disturbing his usually serene
demeanour. After a while Pamela deliberately switches off the
radio and Desmond is caught mid-pace. Undaunted, he speaks
to himself ... or is it to Pamela ... or even the audience?*

Desmond It isn't the sand that worries me, I think that should be
clearly understood — I can cope with the sand ... And indeed
with any insects or flies ... or ... things. After all it couldn't be
worse than high summer on the west coast of ... of ... of ...

Pamela Did you say something, Desmond darling?

Desmond ... with all those midges ...

Pamela Who, dear?

Desmond Midges.

Pamela Which one do you mean? Midge Harrington? An awful
woman.

Desmond Scotland.

Pamela Midge Scotland? Was she one of the Cardiff Scotlands?

Desmond Spoiled every round of golf, I recall. Fearful nuisance.

Pamela The whole family was. Bad enough having to live in Wales, but they would insist on becoming Druids and getting involved in Eisteddfodds ... or is it Eisteddfoddii ...?

Desmond Bitten everywhere I was ...

Pamela They do use such a strange conglomeration of vowels and far too many consonants.

Desmond Even in the ... clubhouse.

Pamela And wear the most unbecoming robes.

Desmond Had to cover myself in that pink stuff to keep the little devils away.

Pamela Calico.

Desmond No, it was camomile.

Pamela No, that's grass, you mean calamine.

Desmond Do I? (*He begins pacing more*)

Pause, as Desmond paces

Pamela Desmond, darling, what is it?

Desmond You said it was calamine.

Pamela No, not *that*, darling. (*With a wave*) This.

Desmond This? Which this?

Pamela The "this" that you are doing so earnestly.

Desmond Doing?

Pamela At this moment.

Desmond I'm pacing, darling. I'm pacing.

Pamela But just why precisely are you pacing, Desmond?

Desmond You should know by now that I always pace when I'm fraught.

Pamela Ah. (*She returns to her magazine*)

Desmond continues his pacing

Desmond (*halting abruptly*) Aren't you a little curious as to why I am fraught? Darling?

Pamela Country weekend house parties are tremendously relaxing.

Desmond Not curious at all?

Pamela It's because the air is so fresh ... virtually unused ... and clean.

Desmond Is it of no concern to you that I am somewhat, if not considerably ... fraught?

Pamela And it's so very kind of Gerald and Evadne to invite us down.

Desmond Do you not care ... about me?

Pamela Frightfully, my darling — your fraughtness — is that a word? — was one of the reasons we accepted.

Desmond It was?

Pamela So you could forget ... and relax ...

Desmond But I can't. I'm far too fraught ... at the thought of ——

Pamela Hush now. Be calm and sensible — they'll never catch up with you here.

Desmond How can I be sure?

Pamela After all, you don't owe them any money.

Desmond That's true.

Pamela And you haven't stolen anything from them.

Desmond No ... I haven't.

Pamela You just signed some papers ——

Desmond (*interrupting with fervour*) I wasn't myself. I'd been drinking ... celebrating ... the business booming ... and I got carried away with the adventure of it all ... the bravado ... the challenge ... the glory ——

Pamela And you joined the French Foreign Legion.

Desmond Sssh! Pamela, not so loud. They could be lurking — waiting to pounce ... and to carry me away.

Pamela It's very warm in North Africa at this time of year, and you burn so easily — remember that weekend in Weymouth last August?

Desmond Technically I'm a deserter.

Pamela Don't they shoot deserters, darling?

Desmond Is it any wonder that I'm fraught? (*He returns to his pacing*)

Pamela But don't pace with such determination, Desmond. It's very distracting. And there's a positive track appearing on the Axminster. It's like a sheep run.

Desmond sits in the chair and fidgets

Don't let your unease show. You'll spoil the entire weekend. Gerald and Evadne will be dismayed — as will their other guests.

Desmond Other guests? Who are they? How many? Do we know them?

Pamela There's bound to be others. It's a house party. People are invited — different people — that's what parties are all about.

The butler, Butters, enters

Butters Forgive the intrusion, madam — but will you and the gentleman take tea here ... and now?

Pamela I think so, Butters ... to avoid the crush later.

Desmond (*aghast*) Crush?

Butters Very good, madam. (*He makes to go*)

Pamela Oh, Butters ... is much of a crush anticipated?

Butters There is usually something of a congestion, madam.

Desmond How many? And who? Do we know them?

Pamela Do you know numbers, Butters?

Butters Mr Fairfax is fond of surprises, madam. We are rarely given warning of how many to expect.

Pamela Something of a bran tub then?

Butters Neatly put, madam.

Pamela And might we know them, Butters?

Butters I feel sure your circles will have impinged, madam ... whoever the bran may be.

Butters goes

Pamela There now, Desmond, no reason to panic.
Desmond Bran? Who bran? What bran?
Pamela Do relax. There's no cause to worry.

Butters enters

Butters Oh one thing I do remember, it would seem that one gentleman is a tee-totaller.

Butters leaves

Pamela Who might that be do you think? Not that frightful dreadful Dinsdale Morton I hope — if he brings his ukulele I shall not be responsible for my actions.
Desmond It could be *them* ... *they* don't drink alcohol.
Pamela Of course they do, Desmond — they're French ——
Desmond Not all of them. That's where the "Foreign" bit comes in.
Pamela I've never forgiven him for the chaos he created at the Watkinsons'.
Desmond What if it is them? It was only a matter of time.
Pamela Not just time, Desmond, it was volume and his lack of ability.
Desmond We must leave ... at once.
Pamela His *Flight of the Bumble Bee* cried out for a good dose of D.D.T.
Desmond There's no time to lose. They're on to me, I feel sure. They have their agents everywhere.
Pamela Darling — do stop worrying, it's the Foreign Legion, not the Prudential.
Desmond I could be shot at dawn.
Pamela Not in Surrey, darling, they'd never get away with it ——
Desmond Come on. (*He makes to go*)

Gerald enters and prevents Desmond from leaving

Gerald (*crossing to Pamela*) Pamela, darling, sorry we weren't on hand to meet you. Good to see you've made yourself at home — have you brought what's-his -name with you?
Pamela It's Desmond, Gerald.
Gerald Of course it is. (*To Desmond*) Hello, old chap.

They shake hands

Have you known Pamela long?
Pamela He's my husband. Do say something, Desmond.
Desmond We're leaving.
Gerald What? Deserting us already?
Desmond Who's a deserter? Who said I was? Who said anything about deserting? It's a lie. An utter lie.
Pamela Pay no attention to him, Gerald. He's a little over-wrought.
Gerald Happens to us all at some time, Pammy. Why don't you go and have a lie down, old chap?
Desmond What?
Gerald Here, look, take a gin and tonic (*handing him one*) and go for a lie down. It's amazingly relaxing.
Desmond No ... we're going ... can't stay ... pressing engagement.
Pamela Try to lie down first, Desmond.
Desmond I've got a very sick aunt ... somewhere.
Gerald Haven't we all, dear boy — if only they had money too.
Pamela Look, Desmond, even if we are going ——
Desmond And we are.
Pamela — there is packing to be done. So why not go up and see to it all. Have a drink, and a rest and ——
Desmond Well, all right. But ... we really must ——
Pamela (*pushing him out of the room*) Go.

Desmond, bewildered, goes

Pamela (*turning*) Gerald!
Gerald Pamela!

A close embrace

Desmond enters

Gerald and Pamela spring apart

Desmond Which room are we in?
Pamela (*pushing Desmond out*) Top of the stairs, first on your
   left ... go ... go ... go.

Desmond goes

Gerald Pamela!
Pamela Gerald!

A close embrace

   This waiting has seemed an eternity.
Gerald I know. We were held up, and then Evadne insisted on
   calling on a chum on the way.
Pamela Where is she, by the way?
Gerald Went straight up for forty winks — tired out after the
   journey, poor old thing.
Pamela Not like you then, eh?
Gerald You know me, Pam, always ... eager ...
Pamela You're so ... stunning.
Gerald Aren't I just?
Pamela And I've missed you terribly terribly. I could hardly
   wait for the weekend to arrive ... so that we ...
Gerald ... could be together once more ...
Pamela You put it all so beautifully, Gerald.
Gerald I try. If only we could spend more time ... together.
Pamela We can, Gerald, we can.
Gerald But what about what's-his-name?
Pamela Desmond.
Gerald That's the one.

Pamela Oh, Gerald, things have moved so quickly — and it could well be that Desmond will be one of them.
Gerald Pamela, what *do* you mean?
Pamela Let me explain.

Butters enters with tea things on a tray

Butters The tea, madam — as you requested.
Gerald Not now, Butters.
Butters No tea!
Pamela Later, Butters, later.
Butters Should I leave the tray, sir?
Gerald Leave the *room*, Butters, just leave the room.
Butters As you wish, sir. (*He makes to go*)
Pamela We'll ring for the tea, Butters.
Butters (*going*) Very well, madam.

Butters leaves the tray on the table and goes

Gerald So what's the news, Pamela?
Pamela Come into the garden, we won't be overheard, and I can tell you the joyous tidings.
Gerald Pamela — I'm all agog.
Pamela I love it when you are — come on.

They exit to the garden

Desmond enters

Desmond (*finishing his drink*) Pamela, I can't remember what you said. Was it right or left at the top of the stairs, and was it first or —— Pamela! Where are you, my darling? (*He looks round for her and rings the bell*)

Butters enters with a teapot

Butters Can I help you, sir?

Desmond Just looking for my wife ... er ... er ——
Butters Butters.
Desmond Butters. I left her here.
Butters And so did I, sir.
Desmond I went upstairs.
Butters I went for the tea ... sir.

Pause. Desmond demonstrates ringing the bell. Butters shows the teapot

Butters Shall I play mother, sir?
Desmond What?
Butters Milk?

Dinsdale Morton enters brandishing his ukulele

Morton Just a spot for me, Butters old bean — parched, I am absolutely parched, thirst like a ship of the desert. (*To Desmond*) Hello, don't I know you?

Desmond responds to the mention of "desert"

Desmond Desmond Borage.
Morton Not "Lumpy" Borage that married old Pamela Anstruther?
Desmond That's the one. She's around here somewhere.
Morton Oh good grief. She loathes me after that fiasco at the Watkinsons'.
Desmond I must go and pack.

Desmond goes

Morton It's all right, I wasn't going to play it ... yet.
Butters Tea, sir.
Morton Thanks, Butters, I'll drink it later — better make myself scarce if old Pamela's about, she'll make one heck of a fuss if she sees my little ukulele in my hand.

Morton goes

Butters is about to put the cup of tea down when he sees his chance and would take a drink ... then fancies it with a tot of whisky. So he adds that tot, stirs majestically and is about to drink when Evadne gives a bloodcurdling scream offstage. Butters reacts, spilling tea, etc. and wiping himself down

Desmond enters hurriedly

Desmond Wrong room! Wrong room!
Butters So it would seem, sir.
Desmond What can I do? What can I say? Who is she?
Butters One suspects it could be Mrs Fairfax.
Desmond Really? Evadne? I didn't recognize her with her clothes off.
Butters I am truly lost for words, sir ... tea?
Desmond (*helping himself to gin*) Another gin, I think.

Evadne rushes in wearing underwear and negligee

Evadne (*melodramatically*) There was a man in my room!
Butters (*after a pause*) A cup of tea? Madam?
Evadne A man! A man!

Desmond turns to her

(*With recognition*) Oh, Desmond! Desmond! (*She clutches him and drinks his gin*) If I'd only known you were here, you could have protected me, been my knight in shining armour — pour me another.

Desmond pours her another gin

We must go and search out this vile intruder. I feel safe with you around, Desmond. (*She drinks the gin*) Pour me another and come on.

Desmond refills Evadne's glass and she leads him off

Butters Will there be anything else ... madam?

But they are gone. Butters aims to drink his "tea" again and laces it with more whisky, stirs it and is about to drink

Morton enters and surprises him

Morton (*sotto voce*) Hey, Butters, old bean!

Butters is startled again

Butters Sir! You surprised me somewhat.
Morton What's going off? I've just seen Evadne leading poor old "Lumpy" up the stairs ... and she wasn't dressed for charades, what!
Butters A misunderstanding I believe, sir.
Morton Well I reckon I'll make myself well and truly scarce — I'll nip back to London before anyone knows I've been away. I'll go through the garden. (*He makes to go*)

We hear Pamela and Gerald from the garden

Pamela (*off*) So that's how it is ... once he is discovered he'll be out of our way for a long time.
Gerald (*off*) Pamela, you're a delight, such a clever little thing.

They laugh

Morton Gosh. Oh grief. It's Pamela Anstruther. She hates the sight of me. I must hide, Butters, albeit briefly, until I can make a sneaky exit. Where do you suggest?
Butters The gun room, sir, perhaps. There's nothing in there of value.
Morton That sounds like me. Not a word — I'll make it worth your while.

Morton goes into the gun room, leaving his ukulele on the chaise longue

Butters tries the tea business again

Gerald enters

Gerald Butters! There you are. A drink ... two drinks.

Butters is startled again

Pamela enters, following Gerald in

Pamela Oh I feel free ... I feel emancipated ... isn't life wonderful?
Butters Tea, sir?
Gerald Gin, Butters ... two gins.
Butters Very good, sir.

Butters gets the drinks as Gerald and Pamela whisper and giggle together

Your drinks, sir.
Gerald Thank you — get yourself a cup of tea.
Butters How kind, sir. (*He moves to the rear to do just that*)
Pamela (*sotto voce*) Here's to us ... Gerry.
Gerald (*equally sotto voce*) Cheerio.
Pamela (*sotto voce*) And our future times together.

They clink glasses

Butters (*raising his cup*) Cheers!

There is an uncomfortable pause as all three drink — Pamela indicates subtly that Butters should be dismissed

Gerald I think we need some more hot water, Butters.

Butters Sir?

Pamela (*firmly*) Hot water, Butters.

Butters Very well, madam. (*He makes to go, retrieving the ukulele en route*)

Gerald Oh, Butters, has anyone else arrived as yet?

Butters Mrs Fairfax did mention a strange man ... in her room.

Butters places the ukulele upstage and leaves

Gerald Strange man? In her room? What on earth can that mean?

Pamela It means that you too are free, Gerald.

Gerald If only I could remember who I'd invited.

Pamela Evadne obviously has been deceiving you, don't you see?

Gerald By jove ... you could be right, you could well be right.

Pamela Nothing now stands in our way.

Gerald But who the devil could it be though, I wonder?

Morton peers out of his hiding place, and quickly goes back, but he is obviously listening. He might even creep out on his hands and knees in an attempt to recover his ukulele — to no avail — and he retreats

Pamela Don't think about it, Gerald, darling. Just accept that all our problems are solved.

Gerald (*unsure*) Mmm.

Pamela Desmond is technically a deserter from the Foreign Legion, and Evadne is an unfaithful wife.

Gerald Mmm.

Pamela I blow the whistle on Desmond and you give the marching orders to Evadne. Nothing could be simpler.

Gerald Mmm.

Pamela Darling ... you do want us to be together ... don't you ... Darling? ... Gerald? (*She goes to him and strokes his face*)

Evadne bursts in. She is somewhat "squiffy"

Evadne Gerald! Oh Gerald! It was awful, absolutely awful —
there was this ... this strange man in my room ...

Desmond enters

Gerald That's not a strange man, that's what's-his-name.
Desmond Desmond.
Evadne I know! I know! I know who *he* is — he's been helping
me search for the ... intruder ... oh Gerald! (*She collapses on
to Gerald weepily*)
Gerald There, there old girl. I'm here ... everything's all right.
Pamela Tell her, Gerald! Tell her now!
Gerald What? Can't you see she's upset?
Pamela It's an act — tell her!
Evadne He was in my room, Gerald. I woke up and there he
was ... and I needed you, Gerald.
Pamela Shall I tell her, then?
Desmond I'm sure there's a very simple explanation to all
this.
Pamela Don't interfere, Desmond — I'll deal with you in a
minute.
Desmond I thought *we* were leaving.
Pamela You're *half* right. Just give me a moment.
Gerald Pamela, this isn't quite the moment, please ...
Pamela (*in exasperation*) Oh Gerald!
Evadne (*weepily*) Oh Gerald!
Gerald Come and sit down, Evadne. You've had a nasty
shock.

She does. He ministers to her

Pamela And she's about to have another.
Gerald (*admonishingly*) Pamela!
Desmond Shall I go and pack?

Pamela Stay where you are!
Evadne I need a drinkie.

Butters enters with hot water

Butters Hot water, madam.
Evadne Gin.
Butters Very good, madam. (*He puts the water down and gets the gin*)
Gerald Thank you, Butters.
Evadne You must find him, Gerald. He was in my room. You know that don't you, Desmond?
Desmond ... I suppose I do.
Gerald Should we call the police?
Desmond No! No! No, don't do that, don't do that, no. Perhaps he was scared off.
Evadne What are you implying, Desmond?
Pamela Oh do stop all this. Why don't you tell the truth, Evadne? You know who it was, this man was there at your invitation.
Evadne What?
Gerald Have any guests arrived, Butters?
Butters Mr and Mrs Borage, sir.
Gerald We know that, Butters, but who else? Who else? Anyone?
Pamela It really doesn't matter, Gerald. You must just accept the fact that your wife was entertaining a man in her room ... and we all know what that means.
Evadne What are you suggesting?
Gerald Well, Butters?
Desmond I don't think we should become involved, Pamela darling ...
Gerald Butters?
Butters Mrs Fairfax says she encountered a man, sir.
Gerald We know that, we know that.
Evadne In my room, in my room.
Gerald But had he been invited?
Evadne Gerald, do you no longer trust me?

Pamela How can he? This is the end, Evadne.
Evadne End?
Desmond Pamela, what are you saying? And why?
Pamela There are things that need to be said ——

Morton sneezes off, from the gun room

All Bless you!
Pamela — and need to be said now.

Morton sneezes again

All Bless —— (*then they realize*)
Gerald What's that, Butters?
Butters Hay fever, sir?
Gerald Who is in the gun room?
Desmond It's them, Pamela. I said they would come and it's
    them — they've caught up with me.
Pamela Let's hope so, it will make things happen quicker. Come
    on, out, let's see you.
Evadne I told you! I told you. I said there was an interloper. I
    said it, didn't I, Desmond?

*Morton emerges dressed in a dustsheet and topee (pith helmet),
with dark glasses*

Pamela Who the devil is that?
Gerald I don't remember inviting him.
Pamela Who do you remember inviting?
Gerald (*to Morton*) Now see here — you, fellow. What do you
    mean frightening my wife in this way?

Morton responds with gibberish

Evadne It wasn't him, Gerald.
Gerald Ye gods — you don't mean to say we have two
    intruders?

Morton speaks more gibberish

Gerald And I do believe this one's a foreigner of some kind.
Desmond Foreign? Where foreign? Ask him! Ask him!
Pamela Desmond, you're letting your fraughtness show.
Desmond Where's he from?
Gerald (*slowly and precisely*) Where ... have ... you ... come ... from?

Morton speaks more gibberish and makes a gesture towards the gun room

Desmond What's that supposed to mean?
Butters I believe, sir, he means to indicate he was in the gun room.
Gerald Do you speak the lingo then, Butters? My word you have such skills.
Pamela Don't be such an oaf, Gerald. He came out of that room for heaven's sakes. Really!
Gerald Did you call me an oaf, Pamela?
Pamela Well, really, I thought Desmond was slow on the uptake but even he ——
Desmond Ask him if there's a lot of sand there, Butters.
Pamela I need a drink. (*She gets one*)
Evadne I'll have another while you're there.

Evadne holds out her glass. Pamela pours her a drink

Gerald I've never been called an oaf before — in my own house.

Morton speaks gibberish

Desmond Sand? ... In your country? ... Is there ... sand?
Evadne Perhaps there's more of them in the house — a whole legion of them.

Desmond What? Who said legion? It was a mistake, a mistake.
I'm not part of it. I'm not. (*To Morton*) Listen ... I ... didn't
... join ...

Morton feigns lack of understanding

Tell him, Butters. He's got the wrong man.
Butters Sir?
Desmond (*firmly*) Tell him ... now!

Butters shrugs and speaks gibberish to Morton, who replies

Gerald Now see here, Pamela. Let's just sort out this "oaf"
accusation. Explain yourself.
Desmond What did he say?
Butters Different dialect, sir. I couldn't quite catch it.

Morton edges to the gun room to make an escape

Pamela Only an oaf would need an explanation.
Evadne That sounds like my Gerald all over.
Gerald I've been called many things in my time, but
never ——
Pamela Me thinks he protesteth too much.
Evadne He's always been a fool, Pamela, with definite oafish
tendencies — surely you realized.
Gerald That's enough, Evadne! Quite enough! In fact it's
more than enough — it's the final straw. Evadne, I have
something of major import to impart. Are you sober enough
to comprehend?
Evadne Say on ... oaf ...
Gerald It's this. (*He clears his throat*)
Pamela I've changed my mind.
Desmond Butters, just restrain that fellow before he summons
his comrades.
Butters (*holding Morton*) As you wish, sir.

Butters and Morton exchange looks — what's it all about?

Gerald There comes a time, Evadne, when a man —— (*To Pamela*) What did you say?
Pamela It's off. I've seen your true self, Gerald. Better the oaf I know than having to break a new one in.
Gerald But Pamela — Pammy — what of our life together?
Evadne Your what? Have you been philimander — philate — have you been canoodling with Pamela?
Gerald You have strangers in your bedroom. Pamela and I have understandings and assignations in the garden.
Pamela Not any more. I now know you for what you are.
Desmond And I was the stranger in the bedroom. It was I, Evadne.
Evadne Desmond, I never realized you cared.
Desmond I don't.
Evadne Pamela, we could exchange oafs.
Pamela But I don't find yours attractive any more.
Gerald And Desmond is committed to a life in the Foreign Legion.
Evadne How romantic.
Desmond I'm not! It's a lie! I'm not and who told you anyway? (*To Morton*) It was ... a ... mistake ... Tell him, Butters. It was a ... an error of judgement ... I demand a recount ... call your men off ... I need a solicitor. (*He sinks to his knees*)
Pamela How neurotic.
Gerald (*weakly*) What about me?
Evadne
Pamela } (*together*) How pathetic!

Perhaps Evadne and Pamela drink together. Morton slips Butters a pound or two

Butters Might I be permitted to allow the foreign gentleman to go, sir?
Desmond No! No! He'll call reinforcements and I'll be carried away ... I could even be shot. Keep him here, Butters.

Pamela Come now, Desmond, it's only a matter of time before they catch up with you. Why not go now with some ... style.
Desmond Style?
Pamela Make a good exit, Desmond.
Evadne He's like Beau Geste, isn't he?
Pamela No.
Desmond (*steeling himself*) Very well. For you, Pamela ... (*To Morton*) Take me.

Morton is bewildered

Gerald Go on, take him, take him. (*He waves them away*)

Morton takes Desmond's arm and would lead him off

Butters Oh sir, one moment. (*He retrieves Morton's ukulele*) You wouldn't want to leave this behind.

They make to finally go

Pamela Stop! Don't move ... I recognize that ukulele ...
Desmond Pamela, the Legion awaits.
Pamela Let it wait. He's no more a member of the Foreign Legion than I am — it's that tone-deaf half-wit Dinsdale Morton.
Morton (*with a strum on the ukulele*) Turned out nice again! Hello, Pamela, old thing.
Pamela Don't "old thing" me. I swore the next time I saw you I'd give you something to remember me by — so come here.

She advances on him and he retreats ... around the room

Morton Must go. Sorry about that, Lumpy, 'fraid I can't press-gang you into the Foreign Legion after all.
Desmond But I'd got myself all worked up to go ...
Gerald I'll give the police a ring. They'll come and collect you ...
Desmond I say, old chap — that's awfully decent of you.

Gerald Don't like to let a brave soul down.
Pamela (*to Morton*) Just let me give you a little something ...
Morton No, it's all right. I must be on my way — I've got a
  booking at the Temperance Hall.
Butters I knew there was a teetotaller somewhere.

Morton goes to escape via the garden

Morton (*as he goes*) Chin! Chin! See you on the Christmas
  Tree.

Morton leaves

Evadne So we knew him after all.
Pamela We did indeed.
Evadne There was no strange intruder then.
Pamela Seemingly not.
Evadne House parties are losing all their attraction.
Pamela I'll drink to that. Butters, be an angel and find some
  more gin.
Butters Very well, madam.

Butters goes

Gerald Yes, I have to say it, Borage old sport, that I admire
  your spirit.
Desmond You do?
Gerald A life in the Legion. By George, it even *sounds* brave
  — you're one of the Bulldog breed ...
Desmond And does it show?
Gerald I'll say it does. And how long have you signed on for?
Desmond How long?
Gerald Yes, how long? When you signed the form. How long
  was it for?
Desmond Isn't it for ever?
Gerald Life, you mean?

Desmond I suppose so. I'll check. I've got a copy here somewhere. (*He rummages about his pockets*) Ah — here we are.

Pamela and Evadne close in to see and Gerald takes the form to read

Gerald By jove ... you're right ... it's life right enough.
Pamela
Evadne } (*together, somewhat aghast*) Life!

Desmond stands very much to attention. Gerald begins to laugh

Pamela Gerald — how can you?

Gerald laughs more

Evadne When Desmond is so very brave.
Pamela Sacrificing himself to the Legion.
Gerald Sacrifice — no how. Legion — no where. He's not joined the Foreign Legion. He's signed the pledge!
Desmond (*grabbing the paper*) What?

The others laugh

  Butters enters

Butters The gin, as requested.

More laughter. Evadne takes the gin but holds it away from Desmond. Ad-lib comments

Gerald That will be all, Butters.
Butters Very good, sir. Oh, there is an army major asking for Mr Borage.
Desmond What?

All fall quiet

There can't be, Butters, I mean I didn't join ... they can't have
come for me. I'm not in the Foreign Legion.
Butters It's not the Foreign Legion, sir. Apparently you volun-
teered to address a meeting at the Temperance Hall — it's the
Salvation Army.

Offstage band recording of "Onward Christian Soldiers"

Desmond straightens up and marches bravely out

The others drink a toast to him

CURTAIN

FURNITURE AND PROPERTY LIST

On stage: Chaise longue
Chair
Side table. *On it*: bell, gin, tonic, whisky, glasses
Occasional table. *On it*: Radio
Magazine (for **Pamela**)

Off stage: Tea things (**Butters**)
Teapot (**Butters**)
Ukulele (**Morton**)
Hot water (**Butters**)

Personal: **Pamela**: watch, cigarette in a holder
Morton: pound notes (in pocket)
Desmond: paper form (in pocket)

LIGHTING PLOT

Practical fittings required: nil

To open: General interior lighting

No cues

EFFECTS PLOT

Cue 1	To open	(Page 1)
	A radio plays music of the period	
Cue 2	**Pamela** switches the radio off	(Page 1)
	Cut music	
Cue 3	**Butters**: "— it's the Salvation Army."	(Page 23)
	"Onward Christian Soldiers" plays	